GRANDMOTHER'S QUILT

To Ruth Griffin —
whose energy is
contagious + Beautiful.
Forward in life — — —
Joos —
  Esther Duffler,
  October, Third,
  North Houghton
  New Hampshire.

Also by this Author:

POETRY:
String of Beads

JUVENILES:
Mary
Rodrigo and Rosalita
The Friends

PLAYS:
Rodrigo and Rosalita (adaptation)

To my ever spirited family—

ACKNOWLEDGMENTS

Quixote, Houston, Texas; editor, Morris Edelson. Also staff editor, Melissa Bondy. "Sounds from Christmas, 1982"; "Gecko"; "Carrying Pole"; "...woman street cleaner"; "On Huangpu River"; "Great Stone"; "ah (Chinese tonal—as a duck calls skyward)."

Penumbra, Portsmouth, N.H., 1979; "Marsh."

Portsmouth Magazine, 1986; "Farmer's Market."

Art Display Poster, Pro Portsmouth Inc., 1984; "Market Square Day."

Poems for the Solstice, editor Marie Harris, Northwood Press; "Christmas Wreath."

Tiny Roads Inside The Cabbage, editors Marie Harris and Deb Alberts, New Hampshire Poetry in the Schools, 1972-1982; "The Loon Calls"; "Sunday At The Unitarian Church"; "Lemon Lily"; "Spots."

re:Ports, 1986; "Winnie Mandela."

* * *   * * *   * * *

Grateful to:

All Skimmilk Farm poets who give and get the best from poetry at the Skimmilk Farm poetry seminars.

Creative Classrooms, Inc., Raymond, N.H. who have included me in their innovative use of performance and study of poetry in the classroom.

Marie Harris, poet and mentor.

Lorraine Ryan, always my friendly critic.

New Hampshire school children and their teachers for the fun and pleasure we've had together with poetry.

Library of Congress Catalog Card Number 88-80081

ISBN 0-8233-0444-2

Printed in the United States of America

GRANDMOTHER'S QUILT

By

ESTHER BUFFLER

THE GOLDEN QUILL PRESS
Publishers
Francestown   New Hampshire

CONTENTS

SEASONALS

TO THE PEOPLE

WHITE LADY OF THE ROCKINGHAM

GRANDMOTHER'S QUILT

GRANDMOTHER'S QUILT

Hangs on the wall
Beside my typewriter. Vivid.

What I would give to
Stay put on her lap,
And smell the full bosomed
Sweetness of freshly ironed
Hand-tucked white shirtwaist
Making ridges into my cheek.
Hang on my arm her sunbonnet
Rosy stained with raspberries from the patch,
Or fill the basket with drops for peach butter,
Won't hurt you, eat all you can eat! Hear her laugh,
And watch her curly wisps of brown hair bounce
    around her
Spunky brown eyes, framed luminous pink. Find the
    quilt square.
I touch it, cheek to cheek.

Off her lap like a lizard. Upstairs to the sewing room,
Third floor, past scary snake-plant,
Quietly. Safe in the sun of her always open door,
Watch her miracle hands turn, baste, decide what
    colours,
Plain and fancy, placed just so, row after row on
    the rack.
Waiting for the scissor-snip to drop a piece,
Nodding her head, *for me*.

I didn't make dolly clothes.
Soaked, squeezed out the dye,
Tinted water to put into bottles to sit in sun,
Move about, in shadows, light, to dream on.
Look up, see them there. Or pull-stitch together
    uneven
Patches, a small quilt to cover found baby mice in a
    heap of
Corn cob fuzz, so naked, shivering in the corner of
    latticed
Wooden shed. Her laughter at *such antics* rings, rings
Uncomprehendingly still.

By the garden walk grew her favorites; a feather bush,
    butterfly
Bush, and a sweet-smelling shrub. Running to the barn,
    they
Tickle my arm. I breathe in flutter with the yellow
    butterfly
Dipping its way on quilted wings. Grandmother
    reaches for my hand.
We are ready for church. She nips two shrub buds and
    hands them to
Our handkerchiefs, folding the spice inside for
    lady-like comfort.
Restless, I slump through the pew hours longing for
    the outdoors,
When with sharp look, her jet trimmed velvet bonnet
    dances my way.
The sweated shrub's tired perfume clings to the quilt.

Sunday parlour.
I'm sitting there in a small cane-seated rocking chair
Waiting. Shiny skin scrubbed. Plain white dress worked
  in pale blue
Embroidery, blue sash; high shoes, the very best,
  no squeaks.
Now they rumble up the lane! Falling-tops, open
  buggies, voices,
Boats of feather-white foam bulge from the horses'
  bitted mouths,
Drop, float, disappear into dark, cool water in the
  wooden trough.
Sucking. Communion; animals and man.
Shep barks. The men walk the land. Sit on the
  split-rail fence,
Talk crops, cattle, prices, "... help,—can't keep them,"
Nip of tobacco, pipe or chew; Grandfather says,
  "Let's go in!"

Women. With their bonnets held or tied, tread
  carefully through the
Grass and up the walk to the front vestibule;
  fringed beads on
Lights with coloured glass. Red carpeted hallway;
  coats, shawls,
Hung on the maple mirrored rack. Hands to heads to
  fix hair,
Grandmother calling, "Come, take any chair." Straight
  woman talk;
Children, canning, truck-patch, carpets, husbands,
  recipes, fancy

Work, quilts! Jealous glances at Grandmother's
   calla lilies
Painted on glass. And flowers made from feathers,
   like a wreath,
Framed, heavy, funereal. Stork painted on silk,
draped
   on the
Easel, folds making its legs appear broken, I'd get up
   and fix it
If I dared.

Listening, smiling, and with tiny wiggling on my chair,
   feeling the
Corner of the prized paisley fetchingly drooped on
   the grand piano.
Peeping toward the cupola wing, patient, waiting to
   be taken by
Hand to gaze at GRANDMOTHER'S WAX FRUIT in its
   shimmering glass
Dome. Every piece she made, even the molds!
Let nothing happen to Grandmother's wax fruit!!!

Men. Here they come, laughing, stomping, scraping
   shoes on the
Iron outside the kitchen shed. Traipsing dirt? Not in
   this house.
Through kitchen mellifluous sweet-sour smells, surge
   together.
Men's arms brushing women's backs; seated,
   skirted legs ready to
Touch a hard thigh, passing rizz-dough, pie, cake—
   chocolate and

16

White—home canned fruit in pineapple molded dishes.
  Pickles,
Coffee, homemade ice cream, winter only this treat,
  packed in
Snow and creek-ice. Homemade grape juice. See the
  cranberry
Square up there? That's my small glass, twice passed.
  Earned.
Guided by arms, snap-cork up, one at a time, I carried
  the cool,
Mysterious, settled bottles from the dark cellar.
  Shivering;
Slime from water-glass preserved eggs as I plunged
  my arms into
The crock, piling the colander full for baking. I look
  at the
Swinging-shelf that moves the mind in seeing
  row—row—row—
Shoo-fly, apple pie—suspended energy in the making.

Shadows of dusk, milking to do, and time to go.
  White linen
Cloth, napkins; lingering pleasure marked. Chairs
  leaned back with
Bellyful men. Women quick of foot, leave to glimpse
  Grandmother's
Latest quilt on rack; her own design. She's proud to
  show the
Stored ones in the chest; first and second best.
  They admire

Bolts of blue and white checked homespun.
   Handed down heritage,
Never used; carefully turned, refolded, and put back
   in the chest.
Creases of time.

First day of school. I look at the quilt
Heart racked.
"Follow your brother, he'll take you there,"
I stumble down the grassy, rutted lane, can't keep up,
I am crying. He hollers, "Come on Goldenrod"!
Funny. How things mesh with the dead.

One whole year I sat. And my teacher loved me.
Miss Minnie Bobb. She had bright red hair. She's
   up there.
See the smallest desk? Mine. I slid in and out;
   how pleasant
To fit just right. Recess on the grass. How I loved
   to play.
Touching, holding fast at the end of the line of
   crack-the-whip,
Falling down, scared, but smiling and on my feet.
   Made my first
Friend as we sat and talked and ate our lunch. We
   compared and
Exchanged homemade bread sandwiches, an apple or
   pear from the
Orchard, or in winter from the cellar barrel, wrapped
   in one of

Grandmother's homespun napkins; carried in lidded,
  small, round, tin
Kettles. My first pencil box! Look there, it's dark
  blue and
Inside a collapsible tin cup! The pencils kept
  sharpened. I
Began to write properly, and sometimes would
  put down a word that
Was a make-up. And I would smile to myself.
  School's out!
Home.

By the end of that year, I was walking home with
  a neighbor.
A boy. We jabbered all the way, and when he left
  down his lane,
Would give my pigtails a pull. Not hard. I rather
  liked that.
My report card shows there right in dead center.
  "I expect it to
Be a good one," Grandmother said. Soon her lap felt
  stomachy,
Slippery. She watched me out of the corner of her eye.

Was that yesterday?
Where have the years taken us?
The quickening comes,
I hang the quilt close.
I stroke it, and notice the colours
Begin to fade with use, sun.

From my window I see that autumn has
Slipped us another season.
The old church bell sings out and the
Vivid and the dead leaves cover the ground.

JOURNEYS

PEACH TREES AND A BIRD

At the foot of the Great Wall
breath loosens for the climb

onto stones pulled, worked
together by men, like an un-
ending dragon moving stealthily,
tail knocking against centuries.

But this day,
eyes light, reach out to
the million blooming peach trees
careening everywhere, hanging to
rocky hillsides as feet plod, plod
upward on the Wall.

Barbarians ... do your glinting poles
tip us a crimson peach?

Comes the bird;
large, strong it glides
to a heavy twigged bowl belly-nest
in the fork of a Gobi wind worn pine;
its feathers, gorgeous—
turquoise .. black .. dark blue .. red.

I pull forth my Mao cap,
tighten jacket,
touch the arm of a comrade.

THE GREAT STONE

Centuries, Lake Taihu held the stone
deep in its water lap. Now loosened,
pulled out, guided ... stands tall
in the garden.

To come upon it is to feel a
scary quest of self
peering upward
through its thin
water-lapped holes
and as a very small vagrant bird
calling to be heard
hollers out
CHINA:
I cannot hold it in.

CARRYING POLE

The carrying pole
appears to rest easily
where it belongs

on the shoulders.

No throwaway energy
the dance begins with
trot-trot of feet,
swing-swing of arms,
body in flow to weight
in balance, yin and yang
light or heavy loads
at its ends.

Shoulders may callous,
veins may rise blue,
blood may weep
without sound.

GECKO

like a laser
down the middle of my spine
memory shoots its
lizardly tongue
zaps death to the fly
high on that wall
as the comet-tail signals
a territorial

and we toast our joy
chew thin slivers of sweet
glazed roast pig's skin
rapt in a closed room
of ebony embroidered in
celestials
white and blue glass
as a grey-green dusk settles
in over the Pearl
of a Guangzhou summer night

... the woman street cleaner
with her white band hat
and long stalk broom
pushes, shoves others' bits
aside with the grace of a
night cat's slow seeking the
left-overs as the pavement
grays when dawn sleeks in
over Wuxi
and like a child in
old face as if to speak
her smile lightens   deepens
on her born smiling face

ON HUANGPU RIVER

sea swallows stringing in
from Shanghai harbour
light our eyes

as your shoulder rubs to mine
for those moments together

our legs jelly
impassioned
leaning to the river

tenderly as a calligraphy brush
with its pointed
wild animal hairs
stroke—stroke the shadows

as we drift in the afternoon
to the cafe next the Peace Hotel

where tables are small
beer warm
and music not felt

for each
thinking something else

FOOD

The cormorant grabs its fish from River Li,
gulps hard to swallow it, but cannot,
as the rope tightens about its thin neck;
vomits forth its catch like an ill child
with nothing much in its stomach.

limitless

whirrrrrrrrrr of thousands of bicycles
coming at me in clouds of dark trousers
and jackets and caps and legs legs legs
up and down up and down speeding over me:
Beijing ... cough hot from the Gobi with
dragon tail cloak flapping my heart

AT A CHINA ZOO

There she sits
FAT MAMA PANDA

alone in a cage

reaches her very furry, beary
hands to you—sings
baaaammmmmmmmmm booooooooooooo

l	climb	b	t
o	climb	a	r
n	climb	m	e
g	climb	m	e
l	climb	b	e
o	climb	o	e
n	climb	o	e
g	climb	o	e

she eats crickle-crackle
...crackle-crickle ....
some milk, some rice ...
gets fatter ... leaves
from bamboo branch; smiles
from tiny eye-shines liquid
brown round shadows. Calls,
talks, sings to you ... ...

MEMO
HONG KONG, CITY HALL, NOON

The exhibit:
Decorative Motifs in Chinese Art.

Mind spelled out by Ming, Qing dynasties,
feet exhausted, City Hall's greensward
a welcome

where

seated on the next bench, a man,
in bare thin black suit, sat erect,
and removed his shoes

which

I noted were black, much worn, cracks
filled with black polish, shined,

when

slowly he raised one shoe, eye level,
spit on his finger, rubbed around
the shoe's new rubber heel. Repeated
—the other. They glistened, dried.

Held at arm's length, his gaze thoughtful;
as one, he brought them close to his chest,
like two toy soldiers, now
eased them onto waiting
black stockinged feet,

then

with care removed a flat pack,
one cigarette, smoked deeply, the butt
disappeared into a very small pipe,

smiled

stood, watched Chinese chess players
nearby, hesitated, moved away.

Brochure in hand, slipped off my shoes,
read ... *versatility of auspicious symbols
further enrich Chinese decorative art ...*

ah
(Chinese tonal—as a duck
calls skyward)

No dead thought here.
Work, work flattens against
wind, dust, hollow sound of
bicycles ghosty black dodging,
never touching.

No casual eye to the hills
wishing as one with two women,
standing, pulling oars of their
boat in rhythm on River Li.
Sampan comes close in to the
water buffalo's legs sucked to mud;
rice.

Noon, quiet time to eat; greens
from the patch, sweet cooked in oil
from the rape seed; broth of fresh
caught turtle; thin slice of chicken,
pork; small seedy orange/apple;
rice.

Exquisite hands sing to tea leaves,
ping, ping to the basket; the whole
curve of the field empties up itself
to Heav'n in wreaths of women.

The sampan carries dawn
on its long body like a
slow easing carp,
head swaying, eyes roving
from the night, gills open,
coming in, nudging itself
home.

... sycamores bend over me tonight,
hold me there on a China road.

EILEEN

New England: the sweater wraps around me.
Honest sweat of Eileen Gallagher leaps out
under the spell of her Inishowen sheep.
She cards, spins, knits in flow ...
like her loyal County Donegal blood
flamed/dark/in water/sky/soil.
Life in season—salmon, lobster,
turf cut in diamonds; new pure wool
touches her fingers, folds her cottage
in warmth to work.

The smell thickens, feeds me, nestles
me down with the nets, mooring ropes,
lobster-claw stitches; the cable is strong.
Excites, pulls, comforts.
Holds the bones of all who hug.

Is it the wind in a sheep's ear I hear?

O MOTHER IRELAND'S BREASTS

The mind stretches its strings
like a harp. Dublin plays.

Have a cup o tea and
speak of Joyce? But I hear

click-click of cheap plastic shoes ...
women speeding out on Grafton Street
Mother Ireland's breasts high.
Do they all cross themselves
passing a church riding the bus?
Wet the ass on St. Stephen's Green,
touch the hair-chested young men
who hand them a crust? Or at
Davey Byrne's pub? The polo mallet
hangs loose at Phoenix Park.
The Liffey is bridged over
with daring new desires.
Does the gold-headed child
know its mother's heart?

Old one ABBEY spirited
away to the EXILES,
panting in a basement
at Newman House; Beckett
crowned and ghosts of them
sung, directed by her.

Ah sweet James, Desmond, Seamus, Tom,
so few women poets?

We rest on Howth ...
let the gorse spread, prick us,
kick the legs and watch the
Irish Sea wash and sing,
listen to sorted, fragmented
Sybilline prophesies
while our lead eyes slap the reins.

THE ANGEL'S ARM

That parochial feel
in the Center, of which
I had none

until Sean pointed, said
*that statue there is where
they blew the arm off
the angel.*

I looked: the arm is back.
O'Connell Street stays black.
Liffey dips on, quiet.

39

ARCHES OF TRINITY

The statues stare back
solid with the millions
of faces locked to them.

In sun, shadow, the entrance
arc draws forth the seed;
worn cobbles unnerve the
spine; rough, O God, rough.
Ages.

Moments. Lie down under
Elizabeth's oak. Lift
the legs to its shaggy bark

Young!

PEAT

it sheds
in my lap

whole it seems

the dark cool feel
the carbon smell
the fossilized nerve-like grass
as withered white hair in decay
cracks open to

a heartsease roll
atop a Dublin hill

SWAMP CREATURES   OKEFENOKEE

Peanut says:
'gator tail and rice fer supper,
Gre'-gran'-ma makin' it,
watch out alligator!

Poet Woman looks to his eyes,
whispers ... Okefenokee
and superbird owl breathes out
its barred feathers like a
striped balloon caught in the
fork of a misted longleaf pine,
stringed loose with Spanish moss.
Owl waits, hungry for breakfast of
'cooter eggs, baby 'gator, lizard,
whatever its head-pin swiveling
neck can see. No jangle in the
swamp

as Poet Woman's small boat works
its way in quiet drift among the
green, garlanded Suwannee. She
touches a hurrah bush, scoops up
handfuls of the cypress black-gold
tannic water for morning tea. Pops
a wild muscadine in her throat for
sweetness. Sings in treble a cas-
cade of birdcalls. The wetlands
quiver in crimson and a yellow
water lily bobs as the run opens
onto acres ... acres of sky-echoed

'prairies of heaven'. Single
leaf of the Cherokee rose, bit of
yellow jasmine waver in light air,
drop seductively

as Peanut raises his paddle
to a near canoe. He says:
... *go back, go back,*
take your lil' dog out boat,
leave bit back or 'gator
shure eat him up,
shure 'nuf eat him up!

Ahead, a 'battery' of *quaking earth.*
Rotted plants, multiples of decayed
microrganisms drop, form gas, rise
as small islands of trembling land.
Boat hangs still. A sixteen foot
rough blackish back of a bull 'gator
rises on bow-legs, slowly turns head
to us, broad snout opens to show sharp-
edged teeth, jewel eyes watching; his
brain, a tiny round hole in the middle
of his head alerts the noduled spine
and saw-like narrow tail as a whip.
He bellows and hisssses, turns away,
settles back on the trembling earth
for sun and sleep

as a single blue heron drops to the
hummocked shoreline; a moment to breathe
its balance, tucks up one leg and

raises us a question. Peanut says nothing.
Poet Woman ripples her hand in the
mirrored water, gently pulls the rubbery
thin stem of the white hatpin plant from
its swaying water-bed and works it
through her tousled white hair

as from opening silver clouds
Seminole chiefwoman Su-wan-nee
removes her feathers, tosses back
her flower cloak and Peanut and
Poet Woman led by a color guard of
dragonflies enter the alchemy
in a cypress bay.

Their paddles touch alleys of
mirrored waters. The cypress
reflect as deserted underwater
turreted castles. Indian camp-
fires banked 4,000 years push
upon the cypress' seedlings. The
peat shivers, and the young ones
begin their climb, close like
bride and groom wordless in love.

500—maybe 700 years later, a
few are still awake. They gasp
for breath sending up knobby and
gnarled knees. Fire, the axe,
drought can kill them off but the
cypress body holds itself gorgeous,
carries it all in age.

Beware. Draped over a gnomed knee
like a hunk of weather-marked rope,
a cottonmouth, its jet-bead eyes
watch to strike and kill anything
that disturbs its quiet.
Drifting toward Blackjack Island,
the white egret tends her nest,
elegant back feathers motionless;
she hears the beat of wings like
rain overhead. Her mate drops
a rain fish.

Passing Honey Island they know
black bear is snoozing among
berry bushes. Peanut says:
*Mornin' he wash his nose,
sniff for fish.*
The current quickens. The pale
green fans of the palmettos seduce
with their long clotted cream blooms.
The handsome red crest of the lonely
pileated woodpecker stuns with its
crown of beauty from the branch of
a sweet bay.
The wood duck drops its inquisitive
head to the mud. To the sky, a cry
of battle: a small red-winged black-
bird thrashes the air in combat with
a hawk; furious in fight, the drama
ends suddenly; both fly as one to
rest on a burned out branch of an
ancient cypress. Sky-diving, the

graceful kite neats its supper;
direct hit on a cluster of whirl-
ing bugs in the thickening sky.

Peanut says:
Night comin'. Time we
don' git lost. I once, yes
... lotsa stars, whisperins.
Hongry for gran'ma's pig-feets
canned so pretty with that
red bayleaf shinin' ...
The indigo night like a soft
blanket begins to descend over
the wetlands. Poet Woman thinks
of the harmless, satiny indigo
snake as it burrows into her
own blue veined hand. Blue.
Blue. Sky-lanterns rim the
Great Basin. Millions of eyes
watch. Okefenokee holds the
tears of the universe.
Poet Woman splashes her breast,
anoints her head in its waters.

DEJÁ: MAJORCA

I was restless for Dejá ... and Robert Graves. He had lived there forty years, writing prodigiously. Urged to visit this dug out village from the side of the Teix mountain, I needed him close. The best way to travel inland to Dejá was by taxi since I did not wish to concentrate on navigating the narrow roads by car. My taxi driver was a gem. He spoke scarce English and I less Spanish but his exuberance matched mine. However, his use of the seat belt was bizarre. Out of town, careening down roads, he loosed it, while on the plains in towns and about the capital, Palma, he carefully fastened it!

We were off down the coast road to Palma (everything goes through the capital), northward through pastoral scenes of shining green pastures holding on their laps plump white sheep nibbling contentedly among orchards of white blooming almendro trees ... ... the thin black tree trunks leaning every which way. "Why is this?" I asked. *The wind blows where it will.*

Now the road began to climb. Ahead was the health-giving, extraordinary village Valldemosa with its Monastery founded by King Martin of Aragon, rebuilt in the 18th c. and finally sold and divided into cells: private property. The love legend of consumptive Frederic Chopin and Amatine Aurore Lucile Dupin (George Sand) dominates. "Were they all that happy living together in a cell one cold winter?" I questioned my driver. He threw both hands off the wheel and making like playing the piano, smiled, "diddly ... diddly ... diddly ... ah, ah Chopin, maestro Chopin ... you know?"

Shouting at him, "Ah! Ah! Si. Si. I do know Chopin, diddly ... diddly ...". Almost grasping the wheel, added, "And George Sand ... suffered, was unhappy here?" He hung his head and drove on without talk.

The climb northward was fantastic with the glistening Mediterranean thousands of feet below. We twisted and turned many bends and wound down slowly into Dejá. The pilgrim was welcomed by a melodious waterfall. Lemon trees with large cadmium yellow fruit hung temptingly from gardens of rock built houses lining the narrow streets. We pulled up to the taxi bar and I invited my gallant driver for a coffee, joined a middle-aged woman with gorgeous black hair, unashamedly greying, tied in pigtail with bright ribbon. She shot me a glance with her black eyes, lighted a cigarette and leaned easily on the long bar. She did not smile. At the other end, a blue-jeaned older gentleman looked quietly and deeply into an early brandy. At a corner table of the long narrow room, a young blonde woman sat trying plaintively to cajole her three-year-old into finishing a glass of milk. She told me later that this was her first look at Dejá, visiting her mother-in-law. Pilgrims of sorts, I mused. The courteous, handsome barkeep smiled ... I felt I belonged there. My driver rose ... "Gracias, Senora ... I will be here at the time of beginning to get dark ... Adios ...". I replied, "Adios ... Gracias, gracias." He bowed, jumped to his car, revved the motor and whizzed off after backing and pawing gracefully the limited road.

And so slowly I began to climb the appearing-going-nowhere streets. No one opened the closed shutters as I rested on a garden wall. A warm sort of courage took

48

me over and from somewhere I began to feel Robert Graves ... he was glad that I had finally come and to let him show me where he lived ... I remembered a line from one of his love poems: *a bright stain on the vision.*

I took the main highway, a mile or so from the village, and there resting on the hillside stood a squarish, ample limestone house surrounded by olive and pine trees. The weird, gnome-like faces of olive trunks stared at me, suspect. The mood was lyrical. Across the road was a glorious slope of olive trees. I knew that hidden among them was a small amphitheatre where he had read poetry and put on plays. I had chatted with two young people on the road who told me, "He had a private path down to the Mediterranean where he walked alone *to sort things out* before returning to his house to write for the rest of the day." The planes of the young girl's face heightened with her smile and in soft voice she said, "... ah Senor Graves, we all loved him and he loved the people of our village ... gentle, lovely man ... ah Senor Graves."

I sat another hour, then fastened an olive twig to my beret, and feeling quite juvenile, skipped back to Dejá for lunch! The Swiss restaurant's gypsy fire stoked with olive wood blazed cheerfully. Perhaps I should stay overnight? I brooded with the sky ... wondered about the time. The mist came.

I must go now to his final earth place. I climbed many, many steps upward through the narrow hemmed in streets to the hilltop *iglesia*. Closed. Behind the church was the cemetery and on stones engraved in grand Spanish style were the names of Dejá's remembered ones.

And then I found him. In the middle of the cemetery, flat
to the earth, a simple slab, simple lettering. I thought
perhaps a young person might have cut it carefully. I read:
Robert Graves   Poeta   1895 -1985. On it lay a long-
stemmed, fresh, deep pink carnation, placed at an angle,
wetted down in the light falling mist. I did not cry. I felt
no sadness, only strength. Only strength. I walked with
care, small rocks on the path, sorting things out.

BUS TO THE TUNDRA

1.

Heavy dew
on the path,
and out of nowhere
Mother Moose squared off,
blocked the way;
black bead-eyes
strung close
stared. Her fat nose
looked wonderful. Her
large leaf ears breezed out
as Baby Moose cozed
against her left leg.

It was two a.m. Twilight.
Our dance began. She tapped twice,
two hoofs forward. No small talk.
I toed, held out my arms
and pirouetted!
The jagged, dark mass backdrop of the
Alaska Range opened. I ran in
wetness, wrapped in grey,
lavender and gold.

2.

I am covered in sweat, slumped in the seat.
The driver hands us cartons of coffee.

We clear dust from the windows of our
  high-sitting bus;
uneasy, as the narrow string of a road unwinds,
marks the way through the grey and green tundra.
We are 250 miles south of the Arctic Circle.

Snowshoe hares run at our heels;
their huge hind feet plop up and down in applause;
another month, they will throw off their dun to
match the first snow. Ground birds pip
in and out from behind rocks, take flight to a
scrubby birch. The plover is here from Hawaii;
  wheatear
from Asia; tattler from New Zealand; all in a hurry
to get their work of mating over with. Grow before
  the
snows or death from a red-plumed fox. But the
  feather—
booted ptarmigan stays yearlong, abundant in love and
cold. Voles and lemmings, startled, lift their lips
showing blueberry stained teeth. Pika, marmot,
ground squirrel rush about eyeing the kitelike jaeger,
off course, rapacious. The golden eagle dives low,
caught in a swift downdraft pushing in from the Alaska
Range. Sun hits the gold-brown of its neck feathers.

A female Grizzly rears up. Sniffs, lopes after her cubs
as they hug downhill in the juicy green into a
muddy melt-off stream. The male is always off
  somewhere.

Pinpoints of white, the Dall sheep stare with
   indifference;
the stab-eyed ram gives us a show of magnificent
   horns.
The scruffy caribou, moose, wolf, lynx, tiny mouse,
   shrew
are all there. The permafrost holds the lupine seed
thousands of years, decides this summer to bloom in
   blue.
Miniscule shrubs bank the road, wave us a small leaf
flutter. The snowy owl sits like sculpture, asleep for a
few hours on the branch of a century old willow.

3.

Snow banners in plumage; clouds move higher ...
   higher.
The bus jolts to a stop. The driver stands and hollers;
There it is. Denali! The Great One!
In sunlight, 20,320 feet of brutal, shimmering white;
the Mountain burns into me.

SENTINELS
by Lake Minnewashta   Minnesota

MINNEWASHTA blinds in white light,
crows circle icehouses,
wind lashes cars into
eyeless snow gnomes.
Silence. Silence in
luminous white virgin earth of ice.
Ojibwa land.

My window shows trees
circling against the sky
holding in their laps
basins of solid ice and snow,
and around the rims small holes
dug into the ice to pull up fish
baited by other fish from short lines
dropped into the icy black waters.

Big snow stopped. Stilled.
Young boy appears. Hollers possessed
who walked on the snow!
OK. It was a dog, just a dog, OK.
He knew why it mattered.

From my window long legs jog on ...
fluttering ...
like snowflaked ice-lace ...

Disc sun stares pure red. COLD.
Here they come!

Sixteen lean, free flowing young,
gliding on graced waxed wings ...
sinews skiing through
feathered snow.
Ojibwa land.

SEASONALS

THE BAIT

is found in
Drake's Island
salt marsh
where tommycods
whirl about like a
woman's yearning
jumps to the man's wave
as his legs undulate
seductively through
sea grass; seive and bucket
in hand to hold bait
his thighs in rhythm
push through deep rooted green
pointed Spartina. He beckons
to the silent woman who watches
his hands cajoling the copepods.
Primal smell rises through the
runs; marsh tinges to aging,
sounds of summer ...
all blanks except
Desire. The woman's nipples
rise. She feels a mounting tide
over sunned rocks.

Two rubber boots toe out
from under the bridge like
young hunting dogs sniffing
salt, sea, bird to ground,

move forward to fluttering
wings in the silvered, hand-
nailed leaning hoary sea shack.

THE LOON CALLS
as a woman drowning

Old Red and Rattlesnake Mts. look
serious and glacial in granite and pine.
A gray canoe heads nowhere on the horizon.
One tuft of an island shoots up
incredibly lost with its wooden cross;
a people lump, a remnant of hope.

The September sun embroiders patterns
in light and dark feathers of the
nineteen loons as they dive for supper;
finally surface without a sound. Thoughts
run on endlessly ....
watching the frosty migrant gull bob-bob
contentedly, satiated with garbage.

The mind now rams. Sticks in a kink as
the loon's human call floats in. Its
open-throated grace, releases the brain
in an unexpected uncluttered revelation.

NEW ENGLAND SUMMER

fog is delicious.
Eat into its solid density.
Stand bare in secrecy
as globules of mist
quiver the body.

The white gull's wing
knocks against the window
of the brain, sweeping on
in sacred silence.

Draw in the taste of creamy fog
... attainment ... attainment ...

Breath is close, hard,
as the riddle begins to solve itself
with a foraging fogdog leaping forth
from the sensible horizon.

MAYTIME

latewinter spring
no smell earth
when
the
smally
orange-black-dot
ladybug
steadies
her
world
down
the
riverbed
of
my
rumpled
arm

MARKET SQUARE DAY

Rain covered us as one
under a sheet. Raincoated arms
swinging and our no-hats hair
looked and smelled like wetted
chicken feathers. The feel of feet
on the open street flooded with
people, no cars, no traffic lights
to watch, we couldn't get enough
of sloshing in the wet. All day
it rained on children's painted
faces, bundles of babies, pots,
plants hanging loose, pepsi boys,
flossy dressed dolls under plastic,
a gundalow, silver makers, t-shirts,
bright patched quilts under cover.
Time to warm ourselves in the
book store. Rest under the tent
with pop/rock pounding.
Everywhere in the air the
wonderful smell of food cooking
close; barbecue ribs and chicken,
beans, burgers, dogs, pasta,
croissants, too. How did you like
fried dough? Drippy mouths chomped.
No one seemed bothered. It was lovely.
We were walkers in the rain. It
rained and rained and rained
on Market Square Day.

WAITING FOR WOODCOCKS
for Charles

Fifteen minutes after the sun goes down,
wait. We wait.

peeent ... peeent ... peeeeeent ...

Where? There!
Rounded brown wings flap
about our shoulders, like
uncertain people closing in.
The cock bird demonstrates.
With a stark, harsh *peeent,*
rises high, then like a helicopter side-slips
down with a melting *bbbwwwdddrrr* gurgle
to the twig nest, in the hush of a
hidden alder-bush. For that moment,
the night holds all together.

CRICKET FROG BAND

Stars one at a time
reach for my hand
lead me to hear
the cricket frog band
fiddle and dee dee
on the bandstand in the
sleepy, murky swamp.

Trees lean down,
vines like kinky snakes
leap, dance to the weird
crickety music
of the nighttime band.

Listen! But do not speak
or the beat will quit cold,
which it did when I called,
Frogs! You frogs! What's the song?

Silence. Sweet, sweet silence.

Coming out of the swamp,
my car becomes a jigging,
glistening, slippery wet,
huge Green Thing.

It is April night.
Bye, bye winter, hello spring.
The tiny creatures tune up,
playing my song.

MARSH

Silent, wallowing, crouched, sea driven waters move
mucking mucous inland marsh.
Looking at it; strange 'staddles' still stand, storm
washed storing bases stacked with sea grass
for survival (relative); animals, man
hanging tight together
nurtured as one with bird, grass, fish,
Crustacea, ducks...gentle ones, resting,
clinging finding

need: pushing tides keeping pregnant wombs of life;
sucking, sorts salting treacle turned,
waiting a reaper's swishing scythe, fishing boat;
content: tap-tapping earth and
sea's exchange, giving life to the seasonal sludge
in footprints, knowing
restraints, high-stepping mind, plunging
to the acid pleasure of its smell, grabbing
nostrils,

raising hairs, moving like tiny copepods wriggling,
signalling semaphore
to power moving steadily with sapping glutty greed
like burrowing ants following
beyond belief. Death begins—
first an ache as cut
tree stump weeps white, grass 'bulled' to
weird heaps, purple blooming

stalk hangs its head, dead, as nuclear fissions hiss
　　plutonium forebodings;
　syllogisms: a surge, dirge begins shaking the jelly of
　　succulent wombs, paralyzing
　soul. Knowing in brief, minds that cannot, will
　　not speak; shuddering,
　　confused, twisted, tortured, like lost
　　children. Fog pleads to an azure blue,
　　　dimming, sinking

as passions burst trying to save, find, hold back the
　　folding fury, throbbing heat's
　deadly tendrils, withering narrowing arteries
　of the living. Swaying in the constant tides
　　undernourished womb
　　losing its grip, the placenta
　　　shrivels, bleeds, sags loose, helpless ... seared,
　　　fouled doomed: marsh.

BACK FIELD GALLERY

Wildness
holds green:
topples
queen's crown
pink phlox
bluebells;
sun strikes
bronzed stalks
thorned rose;
protects
Anne's lace
daisies;
clothes line
swings
dried wash;
sky blue frame—
Picture
NFS.

GOOD FRIDAY NIGHT

quietly
wetted down under
the cool spring moon
listening to the
peepers singing ...
Her hand led me to the stall
of a white, white colt
shimmering,
her long silver nose
like a magnet
touched my face
swimming it with
kisses. kisses. kisses.

MAY   JUNE

lilacs in Portsmouth, N.H.
mauve—white—and indigo

the wind shifts

to the ear-killing drone of
Air Base FB-111 bombers
announcing readiness to death
with carbon ribbons
streaking the sky ...

the wind shifts

· as to the homestead I fly,
stumble on the crumbly stone-
wall, plunge to the fullness
of an old white lilac bush
bent like a cane
leaning next the kitchen door

the wind shifts

and a fragrance drop by drop
touches the wind with the chiming
of tiny blossom bells
glorioso lilaceous
mauve—white—and indigo.

DOWER CHEST

... how to heave out
the pink peonies
here on the dower chest
flower heads dried
wrinkled
over the paisley
with young round stalks and
leaves still green and
eyeing one another
each day
preposterously

ANTHEM

Late sunflowers autumn gold
however they are placed in a
bowl or one by one
hard to arrange a name on
that which is given taken
by hands that throw back
the touch that brings us
together for a few days
deepening the veins
in the groins of our
New Hampshire granite

INTO   winter vapours

manifest: harvest the
thyme, basil, sage,
rosemary, celery, and dill.
Bliss for the hands.

Heavy wind flays open
the huge yellow head of a
final rose.
Ladybug, ladybug curves
her black-dot-orange back
onto my sweater. She carries
death too soon.

Nervous, the thin phallic cactus
is potted tight between firm
stalks of aging bronzed jade;
points its growing head in lust
for light from the west bays.

Applesauce and Sturbridge ginger-
snaps tonight, served with frost.
October gets serious; draws in
the pepper's plump cheeks,
hardens the pumpkin; Lobelia
holds her fire in bright purple,
signals to winter,
better leave well enough alone.

FARMER'S MARKET
Portsmouth   September

sunflowers in your arms gathering smiles.
Walk one to one among stands feeling our
need to touch, feel the earth's roots from
New England's apples, pears, potatoes, late
carrots, cauliflowers, onions, pumpkins,
cabbages, chard, tomatoes; great good all here.
And from the hearth; bread, fruit and turkey
pies, preserves in shining glass, dawn baked
egg-rolls, vinegars, field honeys, herbs;
earth's bounty as frost shakes its winter
cover. Move slowly among the earth growers
... have you missed anything? Carefully sorted
dried bouquets of treasured weeds, Japanese
lanterns, rustles of silver dollars, bright
blooming plants, piles of late sweet corn,
handwovens, ceramics ... ; cheerful pockets
of coming winter. Smiles bring us close under
an umbrella of friendship ... outstretched hands
give joy as we taste homemade English sausage
rolls, fruit tarts, cookies, and cranberry bread!
Not likely to be seen otherwise, selecting
with care bits of reminders of the farm are
cotton-crisped loveliest of New England white-
haired ladies; nodding, understanding,
tweeded gentlemen ... babies in father-mother
arms stroller along among trim tanned legs
of shorts-swinging couples. A companionship.
The sun stills in the coronas and petals of
sunflowers. Reaches each face. Touches mine.

75

OLD

house.
Eat your heart out
with time. Hold hands
squeezing hours around
the place.

Clean up, clear up,
smell it fresh,
empty out the old bottles
stinking of
rot-watered flowers.

BLANKETED

Small tree, branches of bare, black bark
muffled under heaps of folded white blankets.
Harken the stillness.
Harken the dog's bark.
Harken the ewe's bleat.
The chickadee's song on feathering wings.
Dare this day; demand, devour, bend the limbs?
Or await movement of the branch
not bare from its base.

THERE IS NO HURRY.   **Christmas Wreath**

stays. The greens, greyed and out.
Balls and bows stored in tied-tight-together plastic.
The birch Yule log is now wrapped in
"100 Neediest Cases" newspaper.
Shriveled needles hide.

Christmas wreath stays.
It hangs on the heavy wood door
half covering an initialed name plate.
It is fashioned from the branches of the wild grape.
In and out, in and out they go into a round,
tied with purple yarn, threaded
with cinnamon sticks,
natural wheat macaroni and peanuts.

Untamed tendrils stick out from it
in Tiny Tim curls. It will last
and last.

DREAM   CHRISTMAS TOYS

you must be a bit off
not to want to visit
with your family at Christmas.

No.

I am walking with someone, anyone;
take the offered hand.
The grass is smooth and bright green.
We make the time. What we see is light.
LIGHT. Stream and streams of people
moving on and on in brightness; like
Terpsichore, all reach out arms, touching,
undulating, emanating aurae.....

the anyone pulls away leaving me here

to see

two gorgeous bright yellow lions
sitting together high in a tree
on bare branches; cat heads
turning slowly like wound-up toys
ready for giving.

TO THE PEOPLE

LEMON LILY

for Sara Teasdale, died 1933

On
a
long
stem
the
lemon
lily
stands
straight
in
a
narrow
vase
on
the
marble
mantle
looking
at
itself
in
a
beveled
mirror.

CHARLES HODGINS

The air is soft and the worn car
      carries the late summer down a narrow
sea road. Hidden among fragrant tall pines
      stands a small brick chapel.
The entrance is marked by bare roots. Door is
open. Dampness clings to the walls. But this
      Sunday morning hymns warm the lungs.
      And Indian summer creeps in, flushes
forward to enfold and consume a ruby red cross
      suspended above the altar.

Like a rustle of gentle wind his presence lifts,
      he moves in billowing white gown down
the aisle. By the altar beneath the cross he
turns. His face is lighted in grace.

FOR McCANDLESS JOHN PETTY

b. April 30, 1983

To touch a seed
brought to being
by two in need can
never forever now
be selfish. It is
to see the big feet
of him like John
Appleseed; tiny thin
arms; ever moving hands
and star fingers reaching
for something beyond the
woven basket firmament.
We raise our hands to show
less veins knowing that old
arteries will open to
the touch of him.

ROTHKO AT THE TATE

To be there, seized, clothed
in your canvas. The room,
depth of the black, is mine:
spreads to the maroon.

This blood is ours,
holds through me-awake/asleep;
cuts into the bottom,
actually numbed,
sitting on the bench at the Tate.

ROBERT MOORE:
Quaker among fevered few

his wholeness of spirit rises,
shakes us,

his heart, the heat stirs from
his ashes like a Phoenix, fresh,

as we sit in silence
around the Meeting House stove.*

Very tall plumed pines
nod through wavy old windows

as the late sun holds us
benched together.

Few spoken words; tendrils
cut lovingly

into the darkening
of his death.**

* West Epping Friends Meeting House,
  West Epping, N.H.

** Robert Moore, young psychologist,
   killed in a tragic car accident.

ELIZABETH

I found her down a long
rubber floored corridor
like a paved narrow road
to an exclusive club.
Deceptive elegance.

It matters to me that she
knows I'm here. Stand aside,
wait for the pastor to leave.
"Look in on you next week,"
he says without touching her
hand, the bed.

I sit close trying to reach
the hilarious, the exotic, the
tough times that we'd had; I
even plopped my new hat on
her head. Surrender now to
starched nurses, hard, tired,
pulling her to a lounge chair,
forcing a loaded capsule to
her mouth, swooping a box of
soft chocolates within her reach.
Teeth out.

The hour's visit gone. I take
her hand, tears; a moaning
stings the mind as I walk
the long corridor and disappear.

REBECCA

And when I think about
see Rebecca
my eyes widen
who told thee that thou canst see?

To walk the brow of the green
and look up through a tremendous tree
that reaches so far I fall down
backward as I know there is no end
to things I have to say but am
caught in shrift to my world of words
and it is then again I envy Rebecca.

She steadies for flight, takes the turn
on her own gravelled road, travels deep
inside, and beyond, and writes.

The music begins, twists afresh
as her blue 'hand-painted' moons
catch hold of the unseen. Her words
as in a river, eddy about, bank,
grab hold and stick like a leech
clearing our blood.

WINNIE MANDELA

First Day of Summer
New England
I look down in sudden horror
as I pull off miserable bedsocks
worn thin, fling them away
like abscesses; I stare
at my white feet, repulsed.

Heart hit hard with the look
from Winnie's round eyes,
the scar over her eye ...

as I remember Stewart.
He worked the land. Tired at
day's end, washed up at the pump,
laughter, teeth, grin,
reached out to mother
as she placed the small one,
me, in his arms; high to the sky
he sang; *up goes the little*
rubber boot ... ...
still there   still there

and then

Alberta

country school, first grade,
her desk in front of mine,

I watch her pigtails tight,
ribbon bright, starched white blouse.

But at her house, the sweet sick odor
from flung dishwater-laundry-sewage
still turns me

fifty years. What am I doing
this beginning summer's day?

HANA QADDAFI

Today there is no light up
to laughter.
The child is dead.

Early on breathed easy,
touched, felt sun on its
limbs, closed in to a lap
in love, nourished ...
celebrating its time

when one black night
a hard grown lump
spewed down a hot fragment
consuming the child
asleep in bed
to its death.

The child is ours,
cradle it—*rockabye—*
rockabye—rockabye—
place it in a plain box
for us to carry ...

the next time is the next.

HELENE   a century marker

her cane
a hand-oiled wing
flies ahead
skittery a bit ...

give me your arm.

An exchange:
spirited self that
will not quit
gives to all a
renewal
tipped in grace.

BECKETT* relearned

The knuckles knocked
      on the table

The hand raised slowly
      It is too late

The book is closed
      It is too late

The flesh dims away
      The word stays

* Samuel B. Beckett

SURFER   grandson

SCREAM against the ten foot waves
            running the beach
all that was seen; storm lighted head
            and a board.
Sobbing agony of time. Warnings were up,
            he was gone.

Another ten-foot giant and I see him
            topping forth
from out the tube of it, dashed against
            face of it
and gone under. Despair. Will it al-
            ways be so.

THERE: delicious strength he came,
            foam clinging,
pushed onward to the beach, riding the crest,
popping the lip of the wave.

THE BULGE

Brilliance began:
as talk in tenderness; running music;
summer sun worked round Round center,
a bulge swelled forth green
from
six months dead Old Caena plant,
her two stalks bare. Veins cut emptying.
Nude, bold in death from adventuring long life,
she awaited throwing out
when
solid state physics maneuvered,
intuited slowly, and the bulge fledged and
shot forth life ...

nothing is hidden

RECOVERY
for R.T.B.

the bay is a lounge
to see down, way down
to the Mesozoic
which I caress ...
it's a Crustacea,
90 million year old one!

Its tiny dead cells
finely etched for breath
in a seabed then—
now warms my legs

... and from the bay's half-
opened window I look down
upon the flowering yellow-
green fringe of a white birch
and feel suddenly uncluttered
like letting fly an old script.

Hypnotized by a new smell,
I turn ... there's ol' woody
dracaena plant bowing down
to her brash offshoot
as it greens, reaches out with
creamy, perfumed, pointed
tumbling stars.

SUNDAY AT THE UNITARIAN CHURCH

There were no rituals.
The weathered podium
stood at one side of the
dim church parlour, lonely
as the man who leaned on it.

He had no script to read
so did not click on the light.
On his back, a rucksack,
filthy with dried dirt,
waterstain, and use.
Venom; blood flowed from him,
relentless, a sharp
steel blade nicking the calm.

A mantle of Vietnam jungle
dropped over us, as he flung
the bag to the floor and pulled
out a card, and one after another:
Can you feel my sorrow? My
bleakness? The mind with its
hinges loose? This ...
discolored air, breath.
The lushness exchanged for death
... the command to kill. Kill
another human I had not even
talked to, touched? A shot ...
and his voice cried in the
rising mist. Am I back home?

He spoke in monotone, dropping
each card back into the sack;
flapped it shut and left it on
the carpeted church floor
in front of us.

Social hour: hot tea and coffee,
light conversation, trimmed sandwiches.
I asked him, *Where do you store it?*
He said, *In the cellar. Smells real bad
when it rains.*

PNEUMONIA

I am the original script
in that glass case ... like
lofty Don Quixote flying around
waiting for Cervantes to
finish off two scripted lungs.
Breath couples to clear staring
faces mooned down ...

They watch in wonder, disbelief
at the manuscript of my face:
lines written with pointed hair,
despair; *is this a performance*,
they think?
They ease away.

The pastures beneath are still.
The leaves on the yew-tree are
dark in waiting.
Sweated currents bring yellow nights.
Spirit purifies.
I begin to hear the Silence.
I have no fear.

Slowly I scratch,
Kick apart the script,
Break through the glass case,
Make new pages
of unspoken metaphors.

BOSTON BROWNSTONE
for Arlene

Her light step on the unshined
marble-chip foyer slips through
the dulled white heavy door; the
noisy security rod scrapes out
an obscenity; her large purple
eyes smile in triumph, *yes ...*
welcome, welcome ...
We sit in used white wicker pieces
carried safely from *back there*.

In quiet, I think of summer campers
rowed across the Schuylkill fighting
rising flood waters sweeping down over
the river's island. Lanterns from
our shed directed them up through
the meadow into the barn's warm
haylofts. All slept in safety.

I feel this now as she carries her
lantern in daring, like a small fire-
fly in the branches hiding, then
blazing out with courage from years
of 'pin and care'.

Evening: finds her running along
the Charles ... mile at a stretch.

SOUNDS FROM CHRISTMAS 1982

coil in my ear.
The Super 767 idling,
revs and lifts off.
At 10,000 ft. sun
shimmers the brown-
mud squares below like
oiled isinglass mirrors.
A petroleum odour
clings in the crevasses
of my skin. The architect
carefully tests the belly
of the mudflat land as
magnificent contemporary
buildings point the verve
and mix of people like
strong teeth protruding,
chomping at life.
Houston, Texas.

A peek at Infinity:
36,000 ft., the wing of
an angel tosses us a shake,
spews foam over us; the
cherub moon full of laughter
reaches the window and
I remember

Austin. Like an ammonite
the ridges in my heart

deepen. I hunt among the
purple crowned hills,
gnarled cedars and find
fresh courage as I walk the
University campus, step
slowly through the unpeopled
patio of the solemn
Architecture Building
knowing how seeded the
classrooms above.

In a brilliant new book—
*100 Years of Growth,
University of Texas—*
I find him! Surrounded
with his beloved students,
now full circle, he reaches
to his sons, grandsons, grand-
daughters, daughters-in-law
unfolding in his aura.

By God, this is exciting!

My wing tips as a gull's,
takes the curve east, floats
down onto New England.
The ammonite is turned
on its side. Its spiral
horn shows a wetted
freshness.

MUSIC　a fragment of it
for Monique

like a warm moist kiss lingering,
　　my sixteen year
granddaughter's light hand ruffles
　　my white ashes hair,
spilling laughter over us ...

la caresse revivre

SPOTS

I kept watching
the chickenpox nick
on my forehead.
Morning, night and sometimes
at noon, I checked out the
red blotched scar.
I tried everything;
the medicine man's sops,
mud, pine gum, vaseline,
copper penny, sassafras
bark, and cocoa butter.
The scar stared at me!
I felt ugly.

The spot is nothing now
...vanished.
How many years has it been?
Now my teenaged granddaughter
and I walk the worn bricks of
Harvard Square.
My bangs flutter in a sharp wind
exposing my getting along brow.
Little talk as we poke about,
push on. She misses nothing.
Her face of massed freckles
garish in the sun
suddenly stares back at us
from a store window. She looks
solemnly at me and says,
There's a lotta girls with lotsa freckles.

SUCH A LONG TIME   for the

... wedding dress ...
... wedding dress ...

pulled in a roll
from a plastic sack,
designed and stitched
by hopeful fingers,
swinging in front of her
waiting body;
her mouth
like the crescent moon
announces her journey
widening, embracing
the whole ...

GIFT IN AGE

New Hampshire forest
what is that tall tree ...

sit on shadowy granite
in slivers of sun

silence

billions of trees
bud-leaf out
thundering ...

bales and bales of days
interlocked, tied together
with hands swollen ...
the soul nudging for room
until something happens
better
than thought it could
but then I always knew and
something did ...

I DID GO BACK

To look through the gate
   which is broken;
holding my breast ridged
   against it to look upon
all that might have been;
to weep on the architect's
   marble slab that needs
my hand to knead our bread.
   Grey-green leaves of
live oaks shake with the grey-
   bearded mistletoe clinging
hanging on to life however.

GREW UP

walking from Market, Chestnut, Walnut,
Locust, Spruce and Pine south on 15th ...
Philadelphia.
Streets named for trees
in a Greene Countrie Towne ...
Penn and Ben, brotherly of men
whose footprints held to red brick and
Betsy treadled stars upon a striped field
of freedom.

Came back to find
new hucksters to freedom
lining the gutters with pushcarts
hawking clothes; wind billowing dresses,
shirts, trousers like Betsy's flag.
Braziers like warm eyes watching
chestnuts roasting, meats frying,
sundries, junk. Fruits, tempting
for the quick buy. Pick the apple, pear,
grapes, banana ...

Peer into Brooks Brothers immaculate
windows sporting sparingly their cashmeres,
slippers soft enough to swallow ...

We keep at it in
Philadelphia.

WIDOW'S LAMENT

Is there no plug for the sound
pianissimo
like interlacing roots
of the mangrove
it keeps crawling through?

But the rope swing
hangs in the yard.
Sit on it.
Pump hard
to the earth.
Low.
High.
Pull up
and turn over.
Cry out.
Jump off.

Solitaire.

GOING HOME

Tired after a day's work in Manhattan
Christmas Eve, traveling far north, my
jumpy VW gave to the hills their due.
Stopped. A bleak cement shed stood alone
by the road; a launderette. Through the
crusted window, a bundled, drab woman
pushed her too many soiled clothes into
the machine's hole. A drooping
light bulb swayed over her ... *my thoughts*
are not your thoughts, neither are ...
The morning star stared. Finally the car
revived and I pushed on through the
Pennsylvania farmland. Up a dirt road
the hillside, holding firm great boulders,
an 18th Century field stone farmhouse
beckoned in the moonlight. The porch light
was on! That told me that my 92 year old
mother had gone to bed.

Following week, days held us close.
The deep hand-planed window sills
held our tea and coffee cups stacked
in her large dishpan. At times, the
woodstove's banging door was thrown wide
for added warmth which gave our faces a rich
glow as we talked about the future, ours and
the world's! I stroked her hand ... read out-
loud. She whispered, *the angels come close at*
Christmas ... don't ever worry.

And like the sturdy, much used shining tin oil lamp so comfortable in light on her oil-clothed cherry kitchen table, I felt her escape into the soul of a newborn.

REJECTION

The hollow inside feeling begins,
like a dried eggshell, crumbling,
falling apart.

The legs keep walking without direction,
skirting the edge of a precipice.

The mind bears the welt of harsh words,
cries into a cup of alibis.

The hollow illness settles.
Flowerettes of frost
cut the window.

In the time there is,
light begins.

STREET SCENE   NYC

this script of mine keeps surfacing:

panting up the subway steps
53rd and Fifth Sunday afternoon
I cross the street to reunion with
the melody of silence, a shadowy
Reubens and a glorious reredos
in the magnificence of St. Thomas church
to find the massive front doors
LOCKED; open 8 - 9 - 11 a.m.

HOW(EVER)

the sidewalk in front holds us
three deep watching
a painter with large sheet of paper
drawing a portrait of young man
with sword piercing his chest
staring forth over a sound box ...

this is a pastel
and the artist maybe twenty-seven
or so is without arms
a shadowy beard almost spooky under
falling hair which he flings back
to properly see what he is doing
working with only toes and feet
and sticks of colored pastel

broken into small pieces
which his toes pick up
rub and blend creating his canvas
with ease and grace and patience

alms flutter gently into a tall small
narrow rimmed basket

LUNA   hate and love

Huge hole in the dark sock
rising up from the heel of his shoe,
curled flesh of self, rubbed and bare,
the memory of it does not go away.
Cavalier poet. Our need only to
share words?

I do not care, but I do
as his foot with shoe and holed sock
rise higher, higher with the sound of
my sobbing as I reach for that white
fleshed nightmarish moon.

THERE GOES THAT TRAIN

Boston and Maine whistling
for the crossing going north
like strung out alabaster pearls
molded to the tracks with the dust
of those gone ahead,
flying as freshly dipped hair washed
in shadows of sun wind rain rolling
in rhythm swiftly tracking horizons
as ethereal lutes beating strumming out
white grains of gypsum baked minerals
to sky ties setting apart blazoned stars
pearly into the morning.

Siding. I wait.

HATS

Our hats were beautiful
or so each of us thought
that moist spring afternoon
waiting for whatever on the
worn steps of Old Carnegie Hall:
my hat ebulliently youthed,
hers, flimsy-floppy banded
in flowers ... ...
our smiles under those hats
seemed to sweep our faces
together. We laughed.

I have an extra ticket. Join me?

A last Toscanini concert: Brahms.
Consumed, we carried our own fire
without speaking.
At the end she slid me a card
and melted away ...

Late night I remembered
and dug it from my larky bag
and read:

VIRGINIA WOOLF

Still have my rumpled old hat
but this season I seek it out
to take a journey down a
remembered sunlit river.

TWILIGHT

A changing of the guard place:
old eyes questing each other,
a long strung out line of blinks

waiting, startled a little
by clanging, closing of gate.

Hurry, love pilgrims, hurry ...

WHITE LADY OF THE ROCKINGHAM

WHITE LADY OF THE ROCKINGHAM

She was here.

An awakening as fog streaked
with dawn pushed against the
unshaded bays of my bedroom. An
opalescence, like a long stemmed
white iris, hovered in the hallway.
The ceiling seemed to descend
framing the presence of a woman
near. Her purple-grey eyes
incandescent stared down at me.
As if washed in from an opened
sea cask, pungent fragrances spilled
through the room; cardamom, mango,
rosewater, ambergris, cinnamon,
licorice, water-soaked wood ...
This was no grey-hooded apparition.
She spoke, *welcome night woman.*

My eyes embraced the curl of light.
Why was she here? *Who* was she?
What did she want of me?

I was the first live-in resident of
the restored hundred-year-old
Rockingham hotel: soft in New England's
October gold; romantic, guarded by
its four bronzed benignly neutered
lions at its massive front doors.

Three days moved in to a top floor
corner suite, jammed with unpacked
cartons, barrels, tossed clothes,
books and my antique bed, upon
which I lay!

Her beauty stunned. She stood straight
in a long sleeved white batiste
shirtwaist ruffled at the neck,
black velvet bow, cameo. Her
styled, flared black worsted skirt,
below nips of well worn, shined
black buttoned boots, gave her
firmness. The face, pale, so pale,
not young, middle-aged without jowl.
Full dark hair, streaked with grey,
combed neatly, middle part, sides
puffed and caught in low chignon.
She did not smile. I didn't notice
her hands. It was the head and eyes
and mien that overwhelmed.
Merciless stillness ...
I reached out one arm from under
my quilt ... then both arms as if
holding up a cup to be filled.
She swayed toward me ...
she had me alone in this old hostelry,
and I knew that I was about to learn
the story of a strange destiny.

HER CANTOS

I

Chalice of Love

Membranes of mist spin from the sea.
Tides rise on the Firth. The merchant ship
waits at harbour to depart, carrying
provisions to the Colonies. A bonny
eighteen, adventure flushes my face,
raises my foot daringly to the sea chest
on deck of my widower father's ship.
His disciplined nod, *go below*,
and the voyage to Philadelphia begins.

* * * * * *   * * * * * *

Continental Congress—1775 sounds its gavel,
calling together men of energy, purpose.
Women of character and charm lighten the
evenings; gowns in fashion; spirited dining
and chaperoned pleasures. The cup of the
cotillions shines and tips a heady brew.
Across the ballroom I find his sharp eyes,
full lips, deep-cleft chin, tight body,
and legs. Does he see my round arms,
dark curls, hazel eyes? Eight of us
move center; reach, touch, bow, whirl,
retreat. Like the bluebird's wing,
we flutter our happiness, beak, exchange,

then back again to partners. Music flares!
The jeweled buckle of my slipper touches
his boot. Laughter brings mist of his breath
to my cheek; ritual of dance pulls us apart,
then returns him to my warm body, forging
our destiny ... the tide pounds its force
as do the tremors of our hearts. I whisper
his name ... John ... John ...

II

Ubi Libertas Ibi Patria

Stretch and strength. He has it all.
Adventures, like a hard headed salmon
muscles, fights the currents. Sound
ideas, diligence, in command, always
in the brine. Draws a sword for
self, country and liberty.
Citizen of the world, jostles for
recognition, prize monies for coffers.
Privateer. Short of stature, drives
his spirit tall among men; Franklin,
Morris, Hewes, Hancock, Hopkins,
Langdon ... all wait his return,
as do I. And as his rope-scarred hands
press my cheek, I know the next hours
belong only to me. The violet sky enfolds.
Strong gale up the Delaware from the
Atlantic, we push away from the stink

of fish and sweat of men, move on
to the comfort and elegance of my aunt's
salon. Laughter, dancing; the crystal
chandeliers dim toward dawn. Daringly,
he invites me to the privacy of his
lodgings, whispers ...

> *I promise, perhaps to buy*
> *land, an estate in Virginia?*

* * * * * * * * * * * *

Heat of war mounts. Colonies in revolt!
Fervor for liberty bleeds our Scottish veins.
Word comes:

> *The British are coming!*
> *John Paul Jones Esq.*
> *Commissioned First Lieutenant*
> *in the Continental Navy,*
> *warship Alfred; leave Philadelphia,*
> *7 December 1775*

III

Adieu

Philadelphia purple like the waters
that lapped its wharves. In best
fashion: black woolen skirt flared
with crinoline, white batiste
shirtwaist, touch of black velvet;
lilac cape, grey bonnet, dove gloves.
Joyous but pale as he arrives.
He moves to me. Pushes my chin;
next time. Turns to the crowd, nods
to the boatswain and boards the Alfred!
My farewell arm is weak; swallow tears
and take strength from his arm as
he raises the Grand Union Flag
(Union Jack & Stripes) in the ship.
A tremendous cheer floods the dock.
Rattttataaaaaaaatat from the drums,
fierce call of the fifes pierces
the peaceful greening shoreline.
Maneuvered well, sails of the Alfred
billow in grace. Full tide and a
neat north wind moves her down the
Delaware and into the Atlantic.
I will never know why but a silly,
tiny hysterical tune crept out of me:

... sail away o sail away
never, nevermore will he
be me ... my ears hear ...
valley of the bones o the
bones o never, nevermore ...

A comforting arm covers me. My aunt
whispers, *he'll come back, come with me.*

IV

Where Am I?

Friend Betsy makes a flag!
B. Franklin is leaving for Paris!
*Will I please join him to liven
the Court?* Studies await!
Colonel John Langdon invites me
to discover New England. Brother
Woodbury wishes me at Portsmouth,
guest in his new mansion. My aunt
strokes our heather scented sweaters,
longing for home. I'm twenty.
Beaux remind me of gulls ...
why do I wait? Word filters through
that John's ship touches Boston.
No word to me. His venery known,
I cry into my own covered cloud.

* * * * * *　　　　* * * * * *

Greene Countrie Towne farewell!!

129

Discovery

Our passage: Solway Firth, then by
fishing boat through the Mull to
Corsewall Point, Firth of Clyde,
and I am home.
The sheen grows; wrapped in barley
and oats, bleated in love with family
and children, and o so bonnie they are.
I hide in a mix of images. The sea
carves its strength in longing ...
his image dances, makes traceries
onto my legs. Visitor from Paris ...
is there news? His promise,
has he forgotten? What drives
him afresh? Love? Vanity? A
madness sticks like spittle,
closes down the arteries of my heart.
No words to quell the burning;
loneliness like an arctic stream
splashes against my ears, my face.

Run With the Wind

Bright is the day. All erica in bloom.
Pinkish-purple flowers on the heath
tangle my hair in flight. A gull
drops a white feather. I stroke, kiss it,
run to the cliffs slippery in greening moss;
a dot of Union Jack flies welcome
to the harbour; find the ruddy sailor with
his dispatch bag! Breathless, will there
be a missive for me? One by one; he calls
... Miss Maria ... o yes! I clutch it,
thrust it to my pocket, and like a
wobbly lamb free in birth, leap through
the heather, climb to a highest rock,
hold it tight to my throat, sobbing.
Blur not a word, carefully remove the seal:

Dearest,

You will come to me.
Nothing nearer my heart.
All arrangements made
for you at Portsmouth,
New England. My ship
Ranger being built here.
We will rendezvous at the
Rockingham Tavern; guests
of the Langdons until the
Ranger is ready to sail.

Captain (me)! Will expect
you October, whenever find
ship for good, safe passage.
Soon to hold you in my arms,
Your,

John

* * * * * *   * * * * * *

In all whiteness of my spirit ...
the moment returns again ... and again ...
like slithers of shredded silk, she began
to glide away ... I tangled my quilt ...
sat up in desperation, and like a band
tightened about my head, called, pled ...
do not leave ... I must know ... did you
come here to the Rockingham ... did you?

Her head illuminated, she neared, continued:

VII

Affirmation

August in Scotland. Family weepings
fog through the house. The Season
is turning. Bonnie I grow as the
sea chest fills with woolens, bonnets,
gowns and an extra pair of sturdy shoes!
How we will talk, walk, embrace the wind
along New England's coast!

132

Sixty days of high water like flying
sea horses push across the frigate's deck
... chickens below squawk in terror ...
the captain urges me to stay below. But
each dawn, my sea glass roams the horizon
for sea fowl. Thoughts leap ... Land ho!
Land ho! *Will this be Boston? No!*
North we sail. Sun lowers down over
The Isles of Shoals; nine waiting islands
like bobbing heads of beautiful children,
motioning our weary frigate to land.
A tremendous tide thrusts along the green,
deer grazing, many open arms of the
Piscataqua! Camp fires smolder and flare,
but not an Abnaki in sight. Small fishing
shallops bob; few weathered houses, their
tiny feet dip in the river; children shout;
gracefully, the ship's rigging lies quiet,
and the vessel's wood scrapes the pier.
I see him. He strides the wharf, then
in might, leaps to the deck, settles
me in his arms. Tears ... tears ...
we are home? Friends reach in welcome;
Wentworths, Wendells, Langdons, Pepperells
... proper greetings from all.
Protective arm about my shoulders, we walk
the rise of the hill, enter the elegance
of Woodbury Langdon's home.
Laughter and a group of bagpipers
blow open the doors with squeals of
Bonnie Scotland!

I settle into an upstairs corner room.
Sea chest unbound, transform into
lady garments; hold tight to the gleaming
mahogany bannister, descend to a new world.
Sup upon New England's best cuisine,
including venison 'pasty' and finish off
with a wonderful rum punch! In fallen
fatigue, John's arm keeps me to polite hour
... then leads me through the red carpeted
hallways to the corner room.

* * * * * *　　　　* * * * * *

... hailing the late bright moon
sky-dropping away to the sun ...
I sit in the corner chair,
crush his head into my lap.

VIII

Halcyon Days

Discovery of limitless selves.
As the sandpiper splays its feet,
so we mark the coastal sands,
confess our passions: his true soul,
the sea. Mine, a nagging to write;
decide to stay and wait.
Hand in hand, fog teasing our nostrils
with springtime lilac, we walk

without talk to the chapel snugged
close to south mill pond; pull open
the unlocked door, kneel at the altar,
and kiss. We look upon one another,
then, at the hand-hewn wooden cross,
and leave. I am a married woman.
No witnesses. Is it with guilt
I write my aunt:

> ... so happy, John and I
> are committed, well, en-
> gaged. Deciding on a
> plantation, perhaps in
> Virginia; plan to remain
> here while he to sea in his
> gorgeous new ship, the Ranger!
> Yours with much love,
>
> P.S.: I live at the Rockingham.
> John has rooms next door ... frugal,
> well kept, it is his American home.
> Details later. Don't you ever
> worry about your *Maria*

IX

Departure

November, 1777 (the date stays near);
the *Ranger* is ready to sail; a gun fires;
drums, fifes fling out a tune; and John
in his best "blues" waves his cocked hat
to all on shore! Sails square away as a
strong northwest breeze nips in from the
White Mountains. The Piscataqua's dark
fast ebb current pushes its arms around
the *Ranger* and moves her toward the Atlantic!
My tiny white handkerchief is a wet ball,
a forlorn drip on the dock.

X

Subdued December

> Winter is upon this land ...
> Straight-up evergreens hold the wind
> in song, humming along with the seraphim
> ... ...

Friends spark the cold as skates chip deep
the ice on ponds. Heavy booted, I push
through snowdrifts to the harbour waiting
each vessel's dispatch packet. *No word.*
Arms of friendship surround. Stacked wood,
each piece brightens, then drops its ash.

In my corner room I write:

Black night. Now the night wind begins.
And I am alone. It is black night.
Spits of ice pit-pit into the chimney
like patterns of print in sound.
I listen to the frailness
in each even dropping of sleet

like the trapped bird's crystal chirp
caught in the wet chimney of the
bayed room. Waiting out winter's end,
I urge myself to move, speak.
But there is no fire tonight
in this unlit space.

XI

Rumours

Rumour brings word the *Ranger* delivers arms
to Boston. Returns immediately to France?
John Paul Jones receives recognition from
the King. He is at Court! Why am I in
Portsmouth? Cold bites and I write:

... a bone shall not be broken
off the soul as nights consume
themselves in passionate fire
of white ice on my north window-
pane ... how soon to be licked
clean—February thaw.

XII

First Robin

A first robin pulls its tiny legs together
and runs in circles over Strawbery Banke.
Sinew of mind brings me to action.

Dear Aunt,

I am returning to the Continent
... and to John ... ...

Dearest John,

Expect me in Paris sometime late
summer. First, a visit to Scot-
land to see your sisters and my
aunt. Then to you, my dearest.
Greetings from all at Portsmouth.
Your rooms next door shipshape.
My arms around you forever,
Your,

* * * * * *   * * * * * *

I weep farewells ... my face buried
in a bouquet of purple and white lilacs
from next door, it is heigh-ho to sea!
The ship is low with salt fish, timber,
hides ... the Banke is green ... a gull
follows crosswind. I pitch forward,
then go below. Storms at sea fasten to me.
A nothingness ... how many days, o how many,
o how many days ... .

XIII

Solway Firth

St. Mary's Isle. Love encloses Selkirk,
River Tweed. Bonnie younguns' and I
scramble the fens ... blow our hearts
with verse. Wet sweatered arms to the sun
we sing ... sing ... . Suddenly, a
missive from Franklin:

> Hurry to us. We need beauty
> at Court. John fills his coat
> with honours, and prize monies!

Benj Franklin

I leave by next packet. Surprise him.
Heathered down lads and lassies flood
the dock. We hug, call our good-byes
—promise to put thoughts to paper!

XIV

L'Opera

Ecstatic, the box perfumed with flowers,
I hold hands with friends. He is expected.
Décolleté gown exposes my beating heart.
Fanfare ... we rise to the King!
All eyes to the opposite box. Small gilt
chairs tilt easily; the entourage
is being seated. The Countess is placed
by her escort. Stunned! I lurch forward
... it is John! My John! The Countess
touches his arm. He smiles in adoration;
hazel eyes, soft brown hair lean to her.
Music begins. Firm, I must let him know
I am here! Simple. I stand in full mien.
He looks; a bright redness starts up
his face. My handkerchief brushes
Mr. Franklin's shoulder; we depart.
There is no sleep. Daybreak.
Flowers at my door with his newly crested
note paper:

    ... unexpected to see you.
    Sail tomorrow. H.M.S. Drake
    my prize? Hope to return to
    Selkirk land soon.
    Forever yours,

               John.

XV

Depths

A week of terrible, terrible pain, torment.
I cannot leave my room. Work, rework my
agony into words:

> Rejection
> A hollow inside feeling begins,
> like a dried eggshell, crumbling,
> falling apart.
> My legs keep walking without direction,
> skirting the edge of a precipice.
> The mind bears the welt of harsh words,
> cries into a cup of alibis ... .
> The hollow illness settles.
> In the time there is,
> light begins.

XVI

Auras

He is at sea. His words as we walked
the Portsmouth beach lift to me again:

> ... war ... war ... They
> unsheath'd the ruthless blade.
> And Heav'n shall ask the
> Havock it has made.

His own poetry within, a found haven.

Quiet by the Seine with friends, I strengthen.
Blossoms from the countryside drift in
on the wind. And I hear of his triumphs,
despair in death of his men in battle,
adulations and prizes. American Colonies,
Britannia, France, Catherine II of Russia,
all find him useful ... is he a pawn
to their consuming greed? Am I ever there
in his heart? What is it we wish?
Like the returning osprey to nest,
I gather my wings and hasten off
to the lochs of Scotland. The tide
bites into the sand. Days disappear.
My pen smashes words like the high,
white spume rising from gray of storm.
Early summer his sisters hear:

> Hope to return to Portsmouth after
> my fever passes ... very tired these
> days. Tell Maria our friends have
> purchased land for us in Vermont.
> Louis XVI bestows me chevalier!
> We all gather together soon,
> perhaps? Yours,

XVII

Breaking the Light

In joy and pain I feel like a small child's
toy; its paint chips away, tossing, tossing.
I must go to him. His need is mine.
By fast packet, I arrive in Paris.
The concierge of the pension hands me
the letter:

> Patriot friend, John Paul Jones
> died this day, suddenly, and alone;
> rue de Tournon, 18 July afternoon,
> 1792. Signed,
> Paris quarter commissaire, Simonneau.

✶ ✶ ✶ ✶ ✶ ✶   ✶ ✶ ✶ ✶ ✶ ✶

In the intense heat my flesh shrivels
in cold, follows each drum beat
of the grenadiers. So few are there:
his valet, the trades, femme de chambre,
little people, friends still in Paris,
old sailors, the curious of a cortege ...
The hot July evening parches my throat

... forever yours ... forever yours ...

Dust of Paris settles over us. It is
four miles, uphill among rough, winding
streets to the Protestant cemetery
beyond the city. It is finished.
Into the clay he is lowered,
"le célèbre capitaine Paul-Jones."
I cry out ... o the sea ... take him
o take him to the sea ... to the sea ... .

XVIII

What We Already Know

Dear night woman, you are most patient.
The muse continues to give me words.
Seasons move close with sprigs of heather
freshly dried, crushed in the pocket
of a Scots lass in love. I am 45.
Again, it is a hot July day. My basket
holds oat cakes, fruit, cream and
an almost finished tin of maple syrup
from friends in Vermont. I walk to the sea
in the oncoming dusk. Wild the tide
as it mounts the crags ... the Firth opens
to storm ... suddenly, the sun overturns
the clouds, spills colour, and
a lodestar beckons. I slide down ...
open my arms ... am taken by the sea.

＊＊＊＊＊＊　　　　＊＊＊＊＊＊

and so we glide:
sit at times in the corner chair
at The Rockingham; float across
the lawn to his rooms next door.
Think of him as you wish.
And of me ... .

(This poem bears witness to the poet's experience of the
White Lady's presence in her tower chamber. The unfolding
narrative is fiction.)

C O L O P H O N

This book is one of an edition of
six hundred fifty copies
printed and bound at The Golden Quill Press,
in the year nineteen-hundred eighty-eight.
The text is set in a digital facsimile
of a typeface designed in 1540 by
Geofroy Tory's pupil, Claude Garamond,
on command of Francois I of France.
The text paper, Smyth-sewn in sixteen page signatures,
is S.D. Warren's sixty-pound basis acid-free
Olde Style, manufactured at Westbrook, Maine.

This infinity symbol ∞
*represents Golden Quill's commitment to quality paper stock,
which will last several centuries,
and our cooperation with
The National Information Standards Organization, Washington, DC.*